BASICS OF MARKETING

SOURAV DAS

Copyright © Sourav Das
All Rights Reserved.

I dedicate this book to my parents. I am thankful to my mother, Mrs. Tripti Das, the one who has taught me, and made me stand on my two feet and my father Mr. Biswajit Das, who had always been my inspiration to move up in career, and fight towards all the odds in life and move ahead.

Contents

Part 1

Foreword

I hope the book will be helpful to all those people who wants to get a basic idea about marketing and it will, also, be helpful for those students who are pursuing their studies in marketing.

Preface

This book is an introduction to marketing field. It explains the meaning, purpose and types of marketing, with some useful strategies that can be implied to promote direct sales as well as B2B marketing. This book also, explains the history of marketing, who it has emerged and is changed with time. Often, there is confusion between marketing and advertisement, and with marketing and sales. This book also, clarifies the differences between these two terms.

Acknowledgements

I am also thankful to my dearest wife, Mrs. Payal Banerjee (Das), who had inspire me to write this book on marketing and share my experience with you all.

Prologue

About the author:

Sourav Das, an astute & result oriented professional with more than 8 years of experience in Marketing and Sales. He is a proactive manager with demonstrated leadership abilities, strategic planning expertise and problem solving abilities. He has assist senior managers with accomplishing demanding targets by encouraging staff and coordinating resources. He has worked with big companies like RICE Group, UpGrad, SkillEnable, Adamas University, Epitech Infosystems Pvt. Ltd. and Frankfinn. He has also received an award for excellent performance and contribution to the Education Department and Admission Department of and by Adamas University.

CHAPTER ONE

What is Marketing?

The first step is to know the meaning of the word marketing, as without knowing the exact definition we can't really imply it, in our business or work.

What is Marketing?

Any measures taken by a firm to attract an audience to its goods or services through high-quality message are referred to as marketing. With the long-term objective of showing product value, developing brand loyalty, and eventually increasing sales, marketing strives to create standalone value for prospects and customers through content.

Professionals in a company's marketing and promotion departments use advertising to attract the attention of important potential audiences. Celebrity endorsements, attractive phrases or slogans, distinctive packaging or graphic designs, and total media exposure are all examples of targeted promotions.

As a discipline, marketing encompasses all of a company's efforts to attract consumers and sustain connections with them.

Writing thank you notes, playing golf with prospective customers, promptly responding calls and emails, and meeting with clients for coffee or a meal are all examples of networking with future or previous clients.

Marketing, at its most basic level, aims to connect a company's products and services with people who desire to use them. Profitability is ensured by matching items to clients.

This field examines the commercial management of firms in order to attract, gain, and keep consumers by meeting their desires and requirements and creating brand loyalty.

The action or business of promoting and selling items or services, including market research and advertising, is defined as marketing. Today, marketing is an important part of every company's or organization's growth plan. As they attempt to advertise themselves and improve sales of their product or service, many businesses adopt marketing strategies without even recognising it. Marketing is one of the most important components of company nowadays.

When questioned, most people have no idea what marketing is and interpret it as selling or promoting. While these responses are not incorrect, they are merely a component of the marketing process. Product distribution, advertising, designing and generating materials like landing sites and social media content, enhancing customer experience, doing market research, forming market segmentation, and much more are all parts of marketing.

Marketing is a wide term that refers to any strategy that aids a company, brand, or individual in achieving their goals.

Marketing research is the function that links the consumer, customer, and public to the marketer through information—information used to identify and define marketing opportunities and problems; generate, refine, and evaluate marketing actions; monitor marketing performance; and improve understanding of marketing as a process. Marketing research specifies the information required to address these issues, designs the method for collecting information, manages and implements the data collection process, analyses the results, and communicates the findings and their implications.

CHAPTER TWO

The History of Marketing

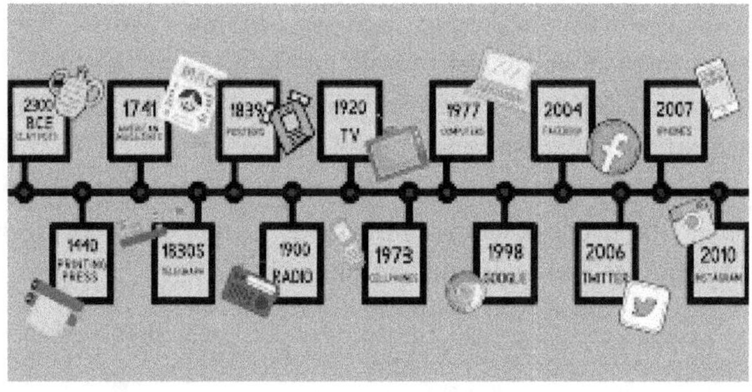

Do you know how marketing has evolved over time?

Not too long ago, marketing mostly consisted of outbound marketing, which meant chasing potential customers with promotions without really knowing if that person was interested in purchasing. Thanks to the digital transformation and the rise of new communication channels, marketing has drastically changed over the years.

To understand how marketing has changed, let's take a look at this timeline HubSpot has assembled showcasing the innovations of this industry.

1450-1900: Printed Advertising

- 1450, Gutenberg invents the printing press. The world of books and mass copies is revolutionized.
- 1730, the magazine emerges as a means of communication.
- 1741, the first American magazine is published in Philadelphia.
- 1839, posters become so popular that it becomes prohibited to put them in London properties.

1920-1949: New Media

- 1922, radio advertising begins.
- 1933, more than half of the population in the United States (55.2%) has a radio in their home.
- 1941, television advertising begins. The first advertisement was for Bulova watches and reached 4,000 homes that had television.
- 1946, more than 50% of the homes in the United States already had a telephone.

1950-1972: Marketing is Born and Grows

- 1954, for the first time revenue from television advertising surpasses revenue from radio and magazine ads.
- Telemarketing grows as a means of contacting buyers directly.
- 1972, print media suffers an exhaustion of the outbound marketing formula.

1973-1994: The Digital Era Flourishes

- 1973, Martin Cooper, a Motorola researcher, makes the first call through a cell phone.
- 1981, IBM launches its first personal computer.
- 1984, Apple introduces the new Macintosh.
- 1990-1994, major advances in 2G technology, which would lay the foundation for the future explosion of mobile TV.
- 1994, the first case of commercial spam through e-commerce is produced.

1995-2020: The Era of Search Engines and Social Media

- 1995, the Yahoo! and Altavista search engines are born.
- 1995-1997, the concept of SEO is born.
- 1998, Google and MSN launch new search engines.
- 1998, the concept of blogging arises. By mid-2006, there are already 50 million blogs worldwide.
- 2003-2012, the era of inbound marketing begins.
- 2003-2004, three social networks are launched: LinkedIn, MySpace and Facebook.
- 2005, the first video is posted on YouTube
- 2006, Twitter is born.
- 2009, Google launches real time searches.
- 2010, 90% of all American households have a cell phone. Instagram is created in October 10.
- Young people between the ages of 13 and 24 spend 13.7 hours on the Internet, compared to 13.6 hours watching television.
- 2011, Snapchat is created, driving even more young users to their phones and fueling the social media app

craze.

- 2012, there are already 54.8 million tablet users.
- 2014, the rise of influencer marketing begins. Users and brands alike begin to realize the power of social media users with large followings. <u>Marketing tools for Instagram</u> and other platforms abound
- 2014, for the first time ever mobile usage outweighs desktop usage. More users are checking social media, reading emails, and making purchases on their phones.
- 2015-2016, big data and marketing automation are explored and used more robustly to advertise to users.
- 2018, <u>video marketing</u> continues to grow, especially with Instagram's launch of IGTV. Video content is no longer just limited to YouTube and Facebook.
- 2019-2020, Move over millennials! Gen Z is the new focus and they have a hot new app: TikTok.

It will be interesting to see where marketing continues to grow. With new world events, like the COVID-19 crisis of 2020 causing millions of people to stay in doors, social media and marketing trends are sure to change, and we'll be right here to track them.

CHAPTER THREE

Purpose of Marketing

Marketing's goal is to constantly research and evaluate your customers, hold focus groups, send out surveys, investigate internet buying behaviours, and ask one underlying question: "Where, when, and how does our customer want to engage with our company?"

Marketing is the process of attracting customers to your business's product or service. This is accomplished by market research, analysis, and a thorough grasp of the interests of your potential consumer. All facets of a business, including product creation, distribution techniques, sales, and advertising, are covered by marketing.

In reality, the primary goal of marketing is to use language to attract customers to your brand. In order to convert consumers into leads, your messaging should be helpful and informative to your target demographic.

The promotion of a company's growth is a key purpose of marketing. Attracting and maintaining new clients is one way to demonstrate this.

To attain these objectives, businesses might use a variety of marketing methods. Matching items to client demands, for example, might entail customisation, prediction, and, most importantly, understanding the proper problem to tackle.

Another method is to provide value to the customer's experience. This may be seen in attempts to improve client happiness and eliminate any issues with the product or service.

Purpose:

Marketing may benefit your company in a variety of ways, but let's look at a few of the most important.

1. Increasing Brand Recognition

This is crucial since it familiarises consumers with your brand and the items or services you offer. It also makes you memorable to customers, who will begin to trust your brand, become loyal customers, and spread the word about you to their friends and family.

2. Traffic Generation

Boosting the number of visits to your site implies obtaining more quality leads (lead scoring can assist with this) and, as a result, increasing sales. This procedure will be aided by an excellent marketing plan.

3. Increasing Profits

Every company wants to boost sales, and marketing can help them do so by implementing methods such as improving their website and SEO, establishing email campaigns, doing A/B testing to determine the best plan for them, and much more.

4. Establishing Your Brand's Trustworthiness

Customer loyalty and repeat purchases are fueled by a high degree of confidence in your brand.

This not only boosts income, but it also leads to positive feedback both online and through word of mouth, which is still one of the most powerful forms of marketing.

5. Metrics Monitoring

When it comes to developing a marketing plan, metrics are really useful.

They not only guide the plan and assist in tracking its progress, but they also provide insight into what can be changed or amended to constantly improve it.

CHAPTER FOUR

Marketing and Advertisement

If marketing is a wheel, then advertising is one of its spokes.

Product creation, market research, product distribution, sales strategy, public relations, and customer service are all aspects of marketing. Marketing is important at every stage of a company's sales process, and it may utilise a variety of platforms, social media channels, and internal teams to identify their target audience, engage with them, amplify their voice, and establish brand loyalty over time.

Advertising, on the other hand, is only one aspect of marketing. It's a paid-for strategic attempt to raise awareness of a product or service as part of the larger aims described above. Simply put, it isn't the only way for marketers to sell a product.

Let's imagine a company is launching a new product and wants to run a campaign to promote it to its existing customers. Facebook, Instagram, Google, and the corporate website are the preferred outlets for this firm. Every quarter, it uses all of these areas to support and create leads for its many initiatives.

It releases a downloadable product guide on its website, uploads a video to Instagram displaying its new product, and invests in a series of sponsored search results on Google that send visitors to a new product page on its website to publicise its new product launch.

How to differentiate between Marketing and Advertisement

Instagram and Google were used for advertising. Instagram isn't often used for advertising, but when utilised for branding, you can build a fan following that's ready for a subtle product reveal every now and then. In this case, Google was obviously utilised for advertising; the corporation paid for space on Google through a programme known as pay-per-click (PPC) in order to direct people to a specific page dedicated to its product.

What was the location of the marketing?

This was a trick question because marketing encompassed the entire process.

The firm launched a three-part marketing strategy that identified its demographic, crafted a message for that audience, and disseminated it across the industry to optimise its effect by integrating Instagram, Google, and its own website behind a customer-focused endeavour.

For those who think that marketing is the same thing as advertising, nothing could be further from the truth. Advertising can certainly be one small part of a marketing plan but it's only one piece of the puzzle. Indeed, it's possible to work from a marketing strategy that doesn't utilize advertising at all.

Marketing can roughly be split into offline and online or digital methods. Offline marketing consists of "traditional" advertising in print, radio, and television marketing, as well as attending events like trade shows, fairs and conferences. It can also include word-of-mouth marketing.

Most businesses will use a combination of online and offline marketing methods. However, these days the balance is shifting more towards online marketing. This is because consumers are increasingly spending more time online and digital marketing offers various advantages in terms of speed, efficiency, and ROI.

CHAPTER FIVE

Marketing and Sales

The Difference Between Marketing and Sales

Sales and marketing are closely linked but they cover very distinct activities in your business.

The sales team doesn't have any say in what the product is or who buys it – they simply take leads and convince them to buy. Employees working in sales must build close relationships with your customers and they need intelligence from marketing in order to do this.

The marketing team *provides* these leads by informing potential customers about your brand and product. They also use customer feedback and intelligence to decide what products to produce in the future or how to change existing products so they meet the customer needs better.

You won't be effective at selling unless the people you are selling to already have some awareness about your brand or product – this is what marketing can do for you.

For a successful strategy, marketing and sales teams need to work closely together and have a unified approach. This ensures that only good-quality leads are passed to the sales team.

You can use a <u>marketing automation</u> platform to align your marketing and sales teams to ensure they're working more efficiently towards a common goal.

Understanding Your Customer

In marketing, knowing your customer is key. In fact, some marketers go so far as saying that marketing *is* essentially the process of understanding your customers.

Marketing should start right at the beginning of your business journey, before your brand even takes form. This initial marketing involves research and learning more about your customers in order to develop a product or service that meets their wants and needs.

This in-depth customer research isn't a one-off marketing task, but one that is continuous. Focus groups, customer surveys, and collecting user data online are all ways that can help you to learn more about your evolving customer base and ensure that your brand is communicating with them in the right ways.

After a particular product or service has been introduced to the market, its success must be evaluated to see if it's meeting customer needs. Marketing also plays a part in customer service and nurturing customer relationships. It's not just about attaining new customers, but also making sure you get the most out of your existing customers and that they stick around for as long as possible.

Digital marketing has opened up a new world of possibilities when it comes to understanding your customers better and building relationships with them.

We now have the ability to collect a vast amount of data about individuals including their demographics, location, shopping habits, previous brand interactions, likes and dislikes, and more.

This data can be used to build a picture of your customers in a way that's much more accurate and meaningful than the traditional "customer avatar" exercise.

Some of the other ways that today's modern marketing technology enables us to learn more about and grow better relationships with customers include:

- Using hyper-personalized messages to speak to each customer on an individual level
- Predicting future behavior with artificial intelligence
- Publishing content that's more relevant to your audience
- Seeing what other content they're engaging with online
- Analyzing brand interactions and optimizing your marketing campaigns
- Automatically staying in touch and nurturing customer relationships after the initial sale

- "Listening in" and talking about your brand on social media – and using it to improve your products and customer service
- Conducting customer surveys easily, cheaply, and with instantly analyzed results

CHAPTER SIX

Types of Marketing

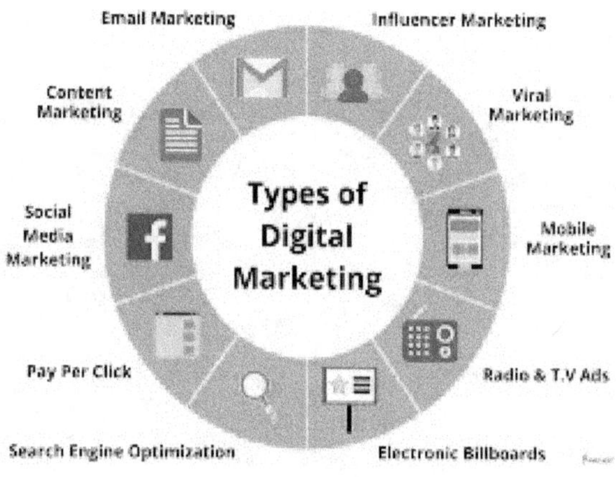

The location of your marketing initiatives is totally determined by where your clients spend their time. It's up to you to undertake market research to identify which sorts of marketing are optimal for establishing your brand, as well as which combination of tools within each category. Here are some examples of current marketing strategies, some of which have shown to be successful throughout time:

Internet promotion:

The entire notion of having a presence on the internet for commercial purposes is a sort of marketing in and of itself, inspired by an Excedrin product promotion that took place online.The technique of improving material on a website so that it shows in search engine results is known as "search engine optimization," or "SEO." Marketers utilise it to attract consumers who conduct searches that indicate they're interested in learning more about a specific sector.

Blog marketing:

Individual writers are no longer the only ones that publish blogs. Brands today use blogs to write about their sector and pique the curiosity of potential customers looking for information on the internet. Businesses may utilise Facebook, Instagram, Twitter, LinkedIn, and other social media platforms to build long-term impressions on their audience. Businesses continue to sponsor stories, photographs, and similar content in the media their consumers read as newspapers and magazines improve their awareness of who subscribes to their print material. While advertisements were previously all that existed, marketers are today investing in the creation and distribution of a wide range of films that entertain and educate their target audiences.

Marketing is not just one single strategy, but rather a combination of many different techniques and tactics. Below we've listed some essential marketing strategies that you should know about.

- <u>Marketing Plan:</u> Discover what a marketing plan is, why you need to design one, and the keys to creating a strong plan. Without a marketing plan, a company or brand can't reach its goals.

- <u>Digital Marketing:</u>Digital marketing is the discipline of marketing which focuses on developing a strategy solely within the digital environment.

- <u>Direct Marketing:</u> Direct marketing is a type of campaign based on direct, two-way communication that seeks to trigger a result from a specific audience.

- <u>Email Marketing:</u> Email marketing is one of the most profitable and effective techniques in terms of return. Naturally, it consists of sending emails to your audience, but make sure to define your segments well in order to be effective.

- <u>Mobile Marketing:</u> Mobile marketing is a broad concept which brings together all marketing campaigns and actions focused exclusively on <u>mobile platforms and applications</u> (i.e. smartphones and tablets).

- <u>Viral Marketing:</u> Having something go viral is every company's dream. Viral Marketing spreads from one person to the next and is capable of going incredibly far incredibly fast.

- <u>Performance Marketing:</u>Performance marketing is a methodology which applies various marketing methods and techniques and guarantees advertisers that they only have to pay for achieved results.

- <u>Inbound Marketing:</u> This methodology focuses on creating valuable content to attract qualified <u>web traffic</u> and work towards the final sale.

There are some other types of Marketing:

Influencer Marketing

According to the Association of National Advertisers (ANA), influencer marketing focuses on leveraging individuals who have influence over potential buyers and orienting marketing activities around these individuals to drive a brand message to the larger market.

In *influencer marketing*, rather than marketing directly to a large group of consumers, a brand inspires or compensates influencers (which can include celebrities, content creators, customer advocates, and employees) to get the word out on their behalf.

Viral Marketing

Viral marketing is a marketing phenomenon that facilitates and encourages people to pass along a marketing message.

Nicknamed "viral" because the number of people exposed to a message mimics the process of passing a virus or disease from one person to another.

Green Marketing

Green marketing refers to the development and marketing of products that are presumed to be environmentally safe (i.e., designed to minimize negative effects on the physical environment or to improve its quality).

This term may also be used to describe efforts to produce, promote, package, and reclaim products in a manner that is sensitive or responsive to ecological concerns.

Keyword Marketing

Keyword marketing involves placing a marketing message in front of users based on the specific keywords and phrases they are using to search.

A key advantage of this method is that it gives marketers the ability to reach the right people with the right message at the right time. For many marketers, keyword marketing results in the placement of an ad when certain keywords are entered.

Note that in SEO, this term refers to achieving top placement in the search results themselves.

Guerilla Marketing

Guerilla marketing describes an unconventional and creative marketing strategy intended to get maximum results from minimal resources.

Outbound Marketing

Outbound marketingis a newer term for traditional marketing coined when the term <u>inbound marketing</u> came into popular use.

In outbound marketing, the marketer initiates contact with the customer through methods such as TV, radio and <u>digital display advertising</u>. It is often used to influence consumer awareness and preference for a brand.

Inbound Marketing

Inbound marketing is marketing in which customers initiate contact with the marketer in response to various methods used to gain their attention. These methods include email marketing, event marketing, content marketing and web design.

One purpose of *inbound marketing*, which includes <u>content marketing</u>, is to establish the business as a source for valuable information and solutions to problems, thereby fostering customer trust and loyalty.

Content Marketing

Content marketing is a technique of creating and distributing *valuable*, *relevant* and consistent content to attract and acquire a clearly defined <u>audience</u>—with the objective of driving profitable <u>customer</u> action.

According to the **Association of National Advertisers (ANA)**, *content marketing* involves various methods to tell the brand story. More and more marketers are evolving their <u>advertising</u> to content marketing/storytelling to create more stickiness and emotional bonding with the consumer.

Some of the different types of online marketing that are available to today's businesses:

- <u>Content marketing</u> – Publishing content in different forms to build brand awareness and nurture relationships with customers. Content marketing is usually thought of as a type of digital marketing but it can also take place offline. Examples of content marketing include blogs, posts on social media, infographics, and video.

- <u>Search engine optimization</u>– Commonly known as SEO, this is the process of optimizing the content on your website to make it more visible to search engines and attract more traffic from searches.

- **Search engine marketing** – Also known as pay-per-click or PPC, with this type of marketing businesses pay to have a link to their site placed in a prominent position on search engine result pages

- <u>Social media marketing</u> – Using social networks like Facebook, Instagram, and Twitter to build relationships with existing customers and reach a wider audience through digital word-of-mouth.

- <u>Email marketing</u>– Sending regular email communications to users who have signed up to your list to build relationships and drive sales.

- **Retargeting** – Contacting existing or potential customers after they have already had an interaction with your brand to get them to come back or convert into a sale. For example, placing an advert on their Facebook feed of a particular product they've looked at on your site.

- <u>Influencer marketing</u> – Using individuals with a high profile and many followers on social network channels to promote your product or service.

These are just a few examples of the most popular types of digital marketing in play today. Each of these methods can be broken down into several other types of marketing and there are indeed hundreds or thousands of different types of marketing covering both online and offline channels.

No business relies on just one form of marketing. On the other hand, unless you're a multinational corporation with a practically unlimited budget and resources, it's not possible to tackle all different forms of marketing either.

To form an effective marketing strategy for your individual business, you must select the types of marketing that will be most effective for you, and form a plan in which they are integrated into a master strategy.

Understanding the 4 P's in Marketing

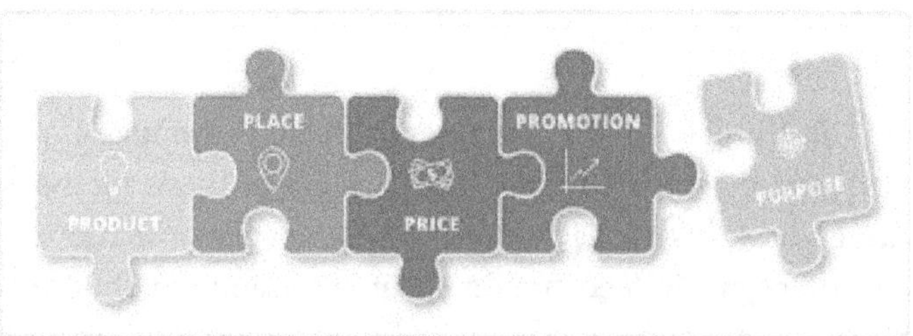

A commonly used concept in the marketing field, the Four Ps of marketing looks at four key elements of a marketing strategy. The Four Ps consist of product, price, place, and promotion.

Product

A product is an item or set of things that a company intends to sell to clients. The product should aim to fill a gap in the market or satisfy customer demand for more of a product that is currently offered. Marketers must first determine what product is being offered, how it differs from its rivals, if the product may be coupled with a secondary product or product line, and whether there are alternative items on the market before they can develop an effective campaign.

Having a product is essential, as it is the foundation of all marketing efforts. A product might be anything that a firm provides to its customers in order to meet their needs. The greatest thing to do is build your product or service on the requirements and motivations of customers, as well as how the product will benefit them, rather than the object's physical traits or attributes.

A product is defined as a bundle of attributes (features, functions, benefits, and uses) capable of exchange or use, usually a mix of tangible and intangible forms.

Thus a product may be an idea, a physical entity (goods), or a service, or any combination of the three. It exists for the purpose of exchange in the satisfaction of individual and organizational objectives.

While the term "products and services" is occasionally used, product is a term that encompasses both goods and services.

Price

Price is the formal ratio that indicates the quantity of money, goods, or services needed to acquire a given quantity of goods or services.

It is the amount a customer must pay to acquire a product.

The price of a product relates to how much it will cost the firm to sell it. Companies must consider the unit cost pricing, marketing costs, and distribution costs when determining a price. Companies must also examine the prices of competing items in the marketplace, as well as whether their projected price point is adequate to constitute a viable option for consumers.

Pricing your products and services is a critical component of any marketing approach. Other elements, such as the margin you aim to attain, are influenced by this component.

What type of customer do you want to appeal to, and how much money do they have? Do you want to go for the high-end or the mainstream market?

The financial objectives of the firm.

What is the pricing of the competition's items, and are there any suitable product substitutes?

Fashions and fads.

Increasing your pricing to offer the impression of higher quality.

Place

The location of a product's distribution is referred to as its location. Whether the goods will be sold in a physical store, online, or through both distribution channels is an important decision. What type of physical product placement does it receive when it's sold in a store? What type of digital product placement does it get when it's sold online?

Strategic merchandising sites might range from an internet store to a network of physical outlets spread over several cities or nations. The purpose of the distribution strategy is to give potential customers easy access to your products/services while also providing a pleasant shopping experience.

Distribution refers to the act of <u>marketing</u> and carrying <u>products</u> to <u>consumers</u>. It is also used to describe the extent of market coverage for a given product.

In the <u>4 Ps</u>, distribution is represented by place or placement.

Promotion

The integrated marketing communications campaign is the fourth P, or promotion. Advertising, selling, sales promotions, public relations, direct marketing, sponsorship, and guerrilla marketing are all examples of promotion.

This refers to all of your marketing and communication efforts aimed at highlighting the advantages of your product or service to the market. This is how you boost your sales.

Promotions are different based on where the product is in its life cycle. Marketers recognise that customers identify a product's price and distribution with its quality, and they account for this when developing a marketing plan.

According to the Association of National Advertisers (ANA), promotion marketing includes tactics that encourage short-term purchase, influence trial and quantity of purchase, and are very measurable in volume, share and profit.

Examples include <u>coupons</u>, <u>sweepstakes</u>, rebates, <u>premiums</u>, special packaging, cause-related marketing and <u>licensing</u>.

CHAPTER EIGHT

Marketing Strategy

What is Marketing Strategy ?

Marketing strategy is the comprehensive plan formulated particularly for achieving the marketing objectives of the organization. It provides a blueprint for attaining these marketing objectives. It is the building block of a marketing plan. It is designed after detailed marketing research. A marketing strategy helps an organization to concentrate it's scarce resouces on the best possible opportunities so as to increase the sales.

A marketing strategy is designed by:

1. Choosing the target market: By target market we mean to whom the organization wants to sell its products. Not all the market segments are fruitful to an organization. There are certain market segments which guarantee quick profits, there are certain segments which may be having great potential but there may be high barriers to entry. A careful choice has to be made by the organization. An indepth marketing research has to be done of the traits of the buyers and the particular needs of the buyers in the target market.

2. Gathering the marketing mix: By marketing mix we mean how the organization proposes to sell its products. The organization has to gather the four P's of marketing in appropriate combination. Gathering the marketing mix is a crucial part of marketing task. Various decisions have to be made such as -

   - What is the most appropriate mix of the four P's in a given situation
   - What distribution channels are available and which one should be used
   - What developmental strategy should be used in the target market
   - How should the price structure be designed

Importance of Marketing Strategy

- Marketing strategy provides an organization an edge over it's competitors.
- Strategy helps in developing goods and services with best profit making potential.

- Marketing strategy helps in discovering the areas affected by organizational growth and thereby helps in creating an organizational plan to cater to the customer needs.
- It helps in fixing the right price for organization's goods and services based on information collected by market research.
- Strategy ensures effective departmental co-ordination.
- It helps an organization to make optimum utilization of its resources so as to provide a sales message to it's target market.
- A marketing strategy helps to fix the advertising budget in advance, and it also develops a method which determines the scope of the plan, i.e., it determines the revenue generated by the advertising plan.

In short, a marketing strategy clearly explains how an organization reaches it's predetermined objectives.

How to Develop a Marketing Strategy

Developing an effective marketing strategy is no quick and easy task, but the basics can be broken down into a few key steps:

1. **Identify your goals** – what do you want your business to achieve in the short and long-term? This may include specific sales figures but also consider factors such as raising brand awareness and your presence on social media.
2. **Market research and identifying your customers** – learn as much as you can about your target customers. Who are they and what do they want and need?
3. **Competitor analysis** – what are your competitors doing in terms of marketing? What products are they selling

and how are they interacting with their customers?

4. **Identify your unique selling proposition (USP)** – what are you doing that makes you a better choice than your competitors? How will your marketing reinforce your brand message?

5. **Choose your marketing channels** – most businesses opt for a blend of online and offline strategies. Again this comes down to understanding your audience – where do they spend their time? What platforms are they likely to trust more?

While your marketing strategy lays out the overall aims and direction of your marketing activities in the coming months and years, your marketing plan will provide the details of the actual activities you'll be carrying out to achieve these goals.

Both your marketing strategy and your marketing plan are keys to your long-term success, whether your business is a small start-ups or a global organization.

Marketing Strategies to Fuel Your Business Growth

Growing a business isn't easy. First, you need a viable idea. From there, you need to discover a profitable niche, define a target demographic and have something of value to sell them. Whether you're peddling products, services or information, getting the word out has become increasingly burdensome. And without the right marketing strategies to fuel your growth, churning a profit and staying afloat is virtually impossible.

However, identifying the right strategies to market your business is often likened to rocket science. How do you get your message to the right audience and do it effectively? How do you boost visibility and increase sales while sustaining a profit with a converting offer? Today, with so much vying for our attention from <u>social media</u>, to <u>search engine optimization</u>, <u>blogging</u> and pay-per-click advertising, it's easy to see why most are ready to pull their hair out.

The truth is that what got you to this point in business is likely not going to get you to the next level. If you're feeling stuck, join the fray. Most entrepreneurs are so busy working "in" their businesses that they fail to work "on" their businesses. As a result of dealing with the day-to-day operations of a company that includes customer hand-holding, supply-chain demands and more, we often neglect to wield the right marketing strategies that will help fuel our business's growth.

What does it take to do that? Simply put, you have to take a step back for a moment. You have to analyze and understand the basic mechanics of your message and how to effectively reach a larger audience without losing your shirt. The secret to all of this? No matter what marketing strategy you use, if you don't have an effective <u>sales funnel</u> and <u>optimize your conversions</u>, you'll just be throwing money away.

What are the best marketing strategies to use?

Most businesses are faced with a conundrum. It's a Catch-22. There's a clear need for increased visibility to drastically improve sales. But in order to get more visibility, businesses have to spend more money. When that well runs dry, what are you supposed to do?

There is no obvious and clear answer to that question that covers all situations. But there are things that can be done today, right now, even on a shoestring budget, to reach more customers without breaking the bank.

However, it all boils down to time. If you lack the money, you sure better have the time to put in the sweat equity.

Either way you slice it, as long as the fundamentals of a sound business are there and you're working tirelessly to build an authentic relationship with the consumer by sincerely trying to add value, then there are 10 go-to strategies you can use to market any business online.

1. Use social media.

You can't ignore social media. That's where all the so-called magic is happening. Some businesses have been built solely on the backs of social media. It can be intimidating at first. Sure. But as you build momentum, you'll find posting on social media to get easier and easier over time.

Of course, you could also hire a social media manager if you have money to burn. But if you don't, just be yourself. Be authentic. Post your thoughts. Post your products. Post anything that you find relevant and useful that would help your audience either learn more about you and your business, or about the industry that you're in.

Use direct messages on platforms like Instagram and even Snapchat or Twitter to reach out to other successful businesses or even to communicate with potential customers who might be looking for your products and services. This is very powerful marketing.

2. Create video tutorials.

One of the most effective ways to get the word out on your business is to create video tutorials. Teach people something useful. Walk them through it. Hold their hands. Step-by-step tutorials are all the rage. The better you are at this, and the more value you provide, the quicker you can boost your visibility, and ultimately, your sales.

Today, YouTube is the second largest search engine in the world behind Google. Whenever someone wants to learn something visually, they head there. You've likely done it yourself countless times. So just ask yourself what you could teach in your business that would help consumers solve some pain point? What got you into business in the first place?

The hardest part? Hearing your own voice playing back and even seeing yourself. Now, you don't have to appear visually on camera, but you'll likely need to be heard. You get used to it over time. But you can't ignore the visibility and reach of YouTube so get out there and start making authentic and useful videos today, right now.

3. Start blogging now.

Sure, you could start a blog. If you don't have a blog for your business, then you need to start one immediately. But you don't just have to blog on your own blog. Most people find blogging mundane because they lack the visibility. The truth is that your blog is going to be like a barren desert unless you know what you're doing.

But this isn't just about posting your ideas on your own blog. You should start authority blogging. Use platforms like Medium to post content. Answer questions on Quora and Reddit. Or get out there onto LinkedIn's publishing platform. These are all authority domains that anyone can post on, which have massive audiences, giving you instant and immediate reach right now.

When you do blog, ensure that you blog effectively. Don't post thin content. Think about adding value. Worried about revealing all your business secrets? Don't be. Give away the farm. Give people so much value that you instantly become an authority in their eyes. This is one of the most powerful strategies you can use to market any business.

4. Understand search engine optimization.

This is an area of marketing that I'm incredibly passionate about. But it's also an area that many people are deathly frightened by. Yes, SEO can be frightening. But it can also be powerful. And when you learn to leverage it and you <u>learn SEO the right way,</u> the sky truly is the limit.

There are companies out there who teach you how to use shady PBNs and other link schemes to "trick" Google. It might get short-term results, but in the long term, you'll land in hot water. You can't take shortcuts with SEO. Just like in business, you have to put in the work and the time if you want to see the results.

Some tips for doing this the right way? Don't spam keywords. Hands down. This is one of the biggest mistakes most people make. Create your content for humans while also paying homage to search engines. But more importantly, ensure that whatever it is that you're conveying is insightful, engaging, unique and adds a tremendous amount of value.

5. Leverage <u>influencers</u>.

Want to get the word out there and boost your visibility on social media without taking years to build the audience? Then you should certainly leverage influencers. But the key is to find the right influencer. You don't have to go with influencers with millions of followers. You could opt for micro-influencers with tens of thousands or even a hundred thousand followers.

The trick? Find the right influencer in your niche so that you're targeting the right audience. It's not just about spreading your message. It's about spreading your message to the right consumer base. If you can do that properly, then you can likely reach a sizable audience for not much money invested when you think about the potential profit it can return.

If your sales systems and products are in place, then this makes sense. If you have an offer that's clearly converting, and it's simply about more visibility, then this is likely the right marketing strategy for you right now. Assess the situation and reach out to influencers and gauge their pricing. Do small tests and see what works, then scale.

6. Build a great lead magnet

So much effectiveness in marketing really does boil down to creating a great lead magnet. I've found that the right lead magnet presented to the right audience can have explosive results. The best way to do this is if you can identify the right pain points and present a solution in your lead magnet, then you're well on your way.

What problem are consumers facing in your niche? What made you get into business in the first place? Ask yourself these questions before building out your lead magnet. The better you identify the problem or pain points at the outset, the better you'll be at actually addressing that with a solution in your lead magnet.

What type of lead magnet should you build? That could either be an ebook, a cheat sheet, a checklist, a video and others. Of course, it's not just about the lead magnet. You have to have a squeeze page with sizzling sales copy to get people to drop into your funnel. But it all starts with a great lead magnet. The better it is, the more effective you'll be at reaching your audience.

7. Use Facebook ads with re-targeting.

One of the most powerful methods you can use to market just about anything these days are Facebook ads. With Facebook, you can reach a very specific audience and you can do it very easily. You can target by interest, age, relationships status, geographic location, and so much much more.

But the trick here to getting great results isn't just about click-traffic. You have to focus on conversions and re-targeting through pixels. If you don't know how to install the Facebook Pixel on your site, then you absolutely must learn how to do this right now. Even if you're not running Facebook ads, you can build your audience with a pixel.

Pixels track everyone who comes to your site, and you can build custom audiences around them. For example, if you post content about how to learn to drive a semi-truck, and you track visitors with pixels, you can then market truck driving certification to people who have already shown an interest in that already because they visited that specific page. And your conversions will skyrocket.

8. Use LinkedIn the right way.

Do you have a video on your LinkedIn profile? Did you know that you can easily add one? Why not take the time to introduce yourself and your business. Link that to your profile description. This is an easy way to passively market your business, and when it's done right, it can lead to shocking results.

If you have lots of connections on LinkedIn and you're not really posting on there, start immediately. You can reach a large audience, especially when your posts go viral. This is a great place to convey the entrepreneurial journey. Talk about your challenges and tell stories. The more effective your stories, the larger your potential reach when you go viral.

9. Create an affiliate program.

Most people don't understand the power of <u>affiliate marketing</u>. Affiliates can provide massive fuel for growth. But approaching the right partners isn't always that easy. You have to have good conversion if you want the bigger affiliate to take you seriously.

I've found that navigating the affiliate minefield can be tricky. It takes persistence and it takes true grit to make it through. Most of us get discouraged after a few setbacks, but you can't allow emotions to get in the way when it comes to affiliate. Build an affiliate program and start reaching out to potential affiliate who can assist you.

10. Use Email Marketing Sequences

Part of any good sales funnel is going to be an email marketing sequence. These are the automated messages that go out to users once they subscribe to your list. Use your email sequence to build a relationship with the subscriber. Be authentic and transparent. And convey your journey.

Use the email responses and clicks to segment your list. For example, if someone clicks on a specific link, they've clearly shown an interest in something. Tag that subscriber to market to them later. If someone buys, tag them as a buyer. Identifying your buyers and the interests of your subscribers is huge for segmenting.

When you do send broadcasts, split test. Split test everything, in fact, You never really do know what's going to be the most effective until you pull the trigger and really test it out. This will help you understand what your audience responds to better, making you a better communicator, and better able to sell to your customers.

B2B Marketing Strategies:

A marketing strategy is your team's plan for grabbing the attention of your target audience and converting them into clients or customers. With people's interests and popular fads constantly changing, it can be a struggle to find new strategies that are interesting and effective. It helps to know what types of strategies are available and how to combine them to create campaigns your audience actually wants to see. In this article, we're discussing topics like:

6 Digital Marketing Strategies

Digital marketing covers all methods and strategies that deal with online media. If you use apps, websites, social media, or podcasts to promote your services, you're using digital marketing. Strategies you can use to reach your target audience through these channels include:

1. Website Marketing

Website marketing is one foundation of online marketing. If you don't have a website, where's your audience going to land when you redirect them from places like social media or an email? Your website serves as a hub for all your content marketing. It's also a place to share information about your business, like contact information, and the products and services you offer.

Increase your chances of getting noticed organically online by making sure your site is SEO compliant with the most recent best practices. You can also optimize a website for conversions, meaning that you increase the chances of people completing a specific action when they get there. Include interactive elements like forms and surveys to entice people to go from casual browsers to qualified leads easily.

2. SEO

Speaking of making your website SEO compliant, that's actually a marketing strategy all its own. Search engine optimization works on tailoring both your on-page content and technical features, like sitemaps, to be more appealing to search engine bots and crawlers. And searchers themselves, by extension. Common SEO strategies include targeting keywords and generating backlinks. This is an easy strategy to combine with all your other marketing techniques to get the best reach and exposure from your content and channels.

Ready to get a leg up on the competition with your SEO strategy? Request your free content analysis report from CopyPress. This report compares your online content with that of your top three competitors. Within, you can find gaps in your content strategy. These areas highlight keywords and topics you can cover in your content marketing or on your website to better capture search intent and provide the information your audience is looking for.

3. Email Marketing

Email marketing is a form of direct marketing done online. It allows you to send messages to subscribers who have signed up or agreed to receive your messaging. Email marketing can be one of the most hyper-personalized communication strategies if done correctly. This strategy allows you to share more than just advertisements with your audience. Once you learn more about your subscribers' needs and habits, you can tailor your email communications to include valuable information, resources, and free materials or discounts.

Plus, email marketing is one of the easiest strategies to track. Programs like MailChimp include built-in analytics for you to watch metrics like open and click-through rates and unsubscribes on every campaign. This information lets you see what your audience likes or doesn't, and you can adjust your strategy accordingly.

4. Social Media Marketing

Social media marketing lets you increase brand visibility with your audience on the channels where they spend time. For B2B companies, this may include platforms like LinkedIn, YouTube, Twitter, and Facebook. Craft your social media strategy in a way that works best for your marketing team and your audience. Use these platforms to share content and resources, engage with potential clients, and answer questions about what you do. The information you share on your social media channels can link back to your website to combine both marketing strategies for more reach.

5. Content Marketing

Content marketing is a type of inbound marketing that uses written, visual, and interactive pieces to provide value to your audience. Digital content is a way to draw people to your website or other marketing channels by offering them something they want to see that solves a problem or meets a need. Content marketing helps establish your brand as a thought leader in your industry. This builds trust with your audience. Whether they're looking to partner with you or purchase from you right now or later, content helps them see why your company is the right choice.

Developing content for marketing works with other channels, like social media, email, and web marketing. You can share your content on all these channels to encourage visits and engagement. The more eyes you get on your content and channels, the better chances you have to gain clients. CopyPress has everything you need to develop your content marketing strategy. <u>Schedule your free call</u> today to discuss your content marketing needs.

6. Mobile Marketing

Mobile marketing is any marketing campaign that you execute on a mobile device, like a smartphone or tablet. Popular examples include app development, push notifications, and SMS marketing. Mobile marketing is another type of digital direct marketing because you can access people right on their personal devices. With things like push notifications, you can choose the dates and times you want people to hear about your promotions or content.

SMS marketing works similar to email marketing, where people opt-in to receive communication. But you may have a better chance of catching them with a text message because people use their phones for both business and social tasks all day long.

7 Traditional Marketing Strategies

Traditional marketing includes all the strategies expert marketers used before the internet and digital marketing became popular. Despite a heavy focus on digital trends, offline marketing isn't dead. For businesses with a local audience, or with an audience more resistant to technology, using a healthy balance of traditional and digital marketing methods helps increase your reach and visibility. Some of these traditional strategies include:

1. Print Materials

Did you know you can repurpose some of your best online content and turn it into print marketing materials? While it may take more time to get the layout right or more money to print physical copies of things like eBooks or white papers, it can be done. And you don't just have to turn your digital content into hard copies word for word. Adapt them to fit print materials that are easy to mail or distribute, such as:

- Business cards: Share your company name and contact information at events like trade shows or conferences so potential leads remember who you are and what you do.
- Postcards and pamphlets: Send advertisements, discount codes, or brief content pieces through the mail or pass them out at community events to interested members of your audience.
- Brochures: These print documents let you share more information about your business, products, or services through the mail or at in-person events. They can also include your website address, social media handles, and links to your online channels for even more connections among marketing strategies.

2. TV and Radio Advertisements

Getting your advertisements on the TV and radio waves are still viable ways to generate interest in your brand. This form of paid advertising lets you share visual and audio promotional messages with your target audience during their favorite programs or on their preferred channels. With the rise of media streaming services like Hulu and Spotify, you can also take advantage of sharing these same types of ads on those popular platforms.

3. Warm Calling

We know, you saw warm calling and your first thought was telemarketers. Then you cringed. But warm calling is more receptive than cold calling, and it's a pretty easy strategy to use with both your digital and in-person marketing. Warm calling is actually similar to email and mobile marketing. Collect a list of phone numbers and names from interested leads and then call them to discuss their business needs and expectations for working with your company. Unlike cold calling, these warm leads want to hear from your company and know to expect a call.

4. Promotional Marketing

Promotional marketing materials are content, events, or swag that make people aware of your brand. They also offer your audience, leads, and current clients incentives to work with your company. Promotions are a popular marketing strategy because there are many different types that fit all budgets and industries. Some popular ones include:

- Contests: Contests help bring out the competitive spirit in your audience. Give them a chance to test their luck or their skills to win a prize, such as a free trial for one of your services.
- Discount codes: These promotions let your customers receive money off a product or service. Discount codes and coupons are a great promotion for companies with a smaller budget.
- Samples: Providing free trials of your services, consultations, or samples of your products may help turn leads into clients or customers if they like what they try before they buy.

5. Direct Mail Marketing

Direct mail marketing is the direct marketing that started it all. And it's still useful today. When the internet came out, email was exciting because it was new. It was a novelty to receive a message online. Now, it's the opposite. Especially when you consider that most tangible mail these days is junk and bills, if that. Direct mail marketing is a way to personalize content for your leads and nurture your current client relationships. Consider sending some of your promotions to your leads' offices or headquarters. Send personalized birthday or anniversary cards to your clients. Sometimes, going retro can help your brand stand out from the competition.

6. Print Media Advertisements

If you've stood in line at the grocery store recently, you know print media is still alive and well. From newspapers to magazines and trade publications, sometimes people just want a break from the screen. And when they do, they turn to tangible materials like these for entertainment. If you have the budget for it, consider getting your advertisements listed in print publications. For businesses with a local angle, you may try to get listed in community magazines or regional newspapers for even more targeted marketing.

7. Press Releases

Press releases are a great way to promote your business in the media. Journalists, podcasters, influencers, and other members of the media rely on them to find out about new events, products, and trends worth covering. You can share press releases with websites, publications, and influencers in your industry. For businesses with a local audience, you can also share them with local television, radio, and print media outlets for coverage.

5 Face-to-Face Marketing Strategies

Face-to-face marketing strategies let you connect with leads and current clients on the most human level. Even if your online and print materials are great, something about a handshake and a genuine connection can take your marketing even further. Face-to-face marketing lets you build and maintain relationships in your niche, industry, and community. Try strategies like:

1. Networking

Networking may sound like a complicated business practice, but it's not. We promise. All it includes is talking with people in your industry to share ideas and information. Networking is a brilliant marketing strategy for B2B companies. Why? Because your potential customers live within your niche. This strategy lets you share what your company does and why it matters with people who need it most. You don't have to make a hard sell because these people are already interested in what you do. Other face-to-face marketing strategies include places and events where you can practice your networking strategy.

Though not face-to-face, you can also network online through social media platforms like LinkedIn, or through events like webinars or virtual roundtable discussions.

2. Community Involvement

Businesses with a local presence can earn face time with leads by participating in community events. Whether you sponsor a charity run through your town or run a booth at the summer carnival, there are plenty of options for brand visibility. Plus, working events like a carnival or a charity event let you talk to people in your town. This may help you learn what they want and need. This type of audience research can help your future marketing campaigns and help refine what your target audience expects from your company.

3. Event Marketing

Both hosting and attending events of your own is also a great way to invite your audience, leads, and clients into your space for face-to-face marketing. Attending conferences and trade shows is a marketing strategy with many benefits, like:

- Increasing brand awareness
- Providing in-person training or education on your products and services
- Creating networking opportunities
- Letting your company conduct market and competition research
- Educating your team members about new products or processes in your industry
- Encouraging lead generation and sales opportunities

4. Workshops and Training

Different from other events that take place in person or online, workshops allow for more hands-on marketing techniques. While you can offer basic demonstrations and training at events like conferences or trade shows, networking is more the central focus. Holding a training session for current clients about your products or services may help them feel more confident in using what you provide. These can also be a great way to let leads experience what it's like to use your products and services before they buy.

5. Public Speaking

Getting some of your most charismatic team members to participate in speaking engagements is another good face-to-face marketing strategy. Who's more knowledgeable and passionate about your products and services than your own employees? Nobody. These events let your company personality shine through in the presentation. Whether you sign up to speak at a conference or a local community event, any chance you can get up in front of your audience and showcase your brand with enthusiasm can help you gain leads.

4 Cross-Category Marketing Strategies

You've probably already noticed many of these marketing strategies may cross over through categories or work together to produce better results. Here are four more strategies that cross through digital, traditional, and face-to-face marketing bounds to get your best returns:

1. Relationship Marketing

Every time you connect with a lead, you're creating a new relationship. These relationships link both you and the lead through every stage of the sales funnel. Then, when they finally become clients, you work to maintain these relationships so they stay satisfied and remain clients over time. Companies that foster positive relationships with their clients may see more sales, more frequent sales, or higher referral rates from clients.

Relationship marketing doesn't have to be hard or time-consuming. Introducing incentives like client referral programs or personalized content may work in some industries. Others may benefit from sharing regular client surveys and asking for feedback, then implementing it into their business plan. For example, at CopyPress, we run our proprietary content management system (CMS), Dante, in-house. This allows us to take client feedback and make changes based on what our partners really need from the service.

2. Partnerships

Partnering with other businesses in your industry may open more opportunities for marketing across disciplines. Working with influencers may help increase your reach for social media marketing. Working with other local companies to host an event may strengthen the interest or economy throughout your entire business district. This may lead not just to more sales, but also to more job stability.

3. Digital Publishing

Thanks to digital publishing, it's easier now than ever to create your own publications. Whether you want to create stunning eBooks online or a print newsletter, the options are available. Creating your own digital publications helps establish you as a thought leader in your industry. It may also be easier to do this yourself or work with a dedicated agency like CopyPress for your digital publication and content needs rather than paying for campaigns with other established outlets like newspapers and magazines.

4. Guerilla Marketing

The term guerilla means inventive and unconventional. In marketing, this type of strategy really forces you to be innovative to increase your leads and boost sales. Guerilla marketing tactics are often low-budget, creative, and draw sizeable crowds. They're effective because they stand out. They're different or amusing, and that often makes them memorable or a publicity draw. While guerilla marketing might not be something you do all the time, it is an excellent strategy to remember if you really want to make a statement.

Competition Strategy - Dealing with the Competition

Consumer and business markets have distinct characteristics by which they function. Earlier, importance was given mainly in understanding customer and their business. But in this age of technology and globalization companies cannot afford to ignore competition.

Many companies are lowering their cost by outsourcing production to Asian countries. Companies must keep an eye on strategies and marketing program undertaken by competitors, to remain successful.

Michael Porter's five force model is appropriate in identifying competitive forces, which affect business in any given environment. These five forces are the threat of companies from same segment, threat of new entrants in the segment, threat from substitute products, threat from the increase in consumer's bargaining power and threat from supplier's bargaining power. If in the same segment there are too many players, if the segment is reaching saturation, if no further scope of expansion than to continue operation is difficult for the company. If the entry barrier are few and far than it makes easy for companies to enter, making segment un-attractive but if the entry barriers are tough than the company is better off in entering the segment.

Substitute products are big threat and limit scope of a price increase. If consumers are better organized, have a choice in terms of product available and can create pressure on profits, making segment un-attractive. Similarly, if suppliers are better organized, less in number and supply is a key raw material for final output than also segment is unattractive.

Dealing with threats is one thing but if companies are not able to identify their competition than it can cause serious consequences. In recent years technology and internet have change the way business is conducted. Many companies were caught napping with respect to competition coming from the internet. Retailers like Wal-Mart and Target are facing competition from online retailer Amazon.com. Companies see competition in a direct format. This direct format consists of industry structure, number of players, entry-exit barriers, business model and ability to globalize. Market looks at competition in much more holistic manner where different products can satisfy a similar need. For example, for teens fashion can be explained by apparel to a music player, so with limited budget choice can only be one. Market approach increases the number of competitor in a real and abstract manner.

Companies after going through the process of identifying competition, also need to do in-depth analyze in terms of nature, strategy, strength, weakness and operation pattern. Companies following similar strategy need to group existing player in a matrix of product offering. For example, in the laptop market, apple is on the high end where as Dell offers low end models.

Companies need to understand competitor's motive and goal to be in the market. US companies believe in shareholder value where as Japanese companies believe in market share. Next companies need to understand competitor's strength and weakness. For example, GM has good reach in USA but its weakness is quality where as Toyota does not have extensive dealer network but offers quality. Competitor's operating pattern also need careful study like competitor's action in the face of challenge to their position in the market.

To deal with competition companies need to design an intelligence system. Companies need to identify parameters which will help in analyzing the competition. It is then followed by gathering information for which source and methodology have to be finalized. Once the information is collected it has to be analyzed and sent to appropriate decision makers to act upon. As there are cost involved in design and maintaining such system, some companies give out contracts to companies which specialize in intelligence gathering activity.

The information from system is helpful in designing marketing strategies. Marketing strategy evolve depending on company position in the market. Market leaders, market challenger, market follower and niche players are four types of position strategy companies follow.

Dealing with competition is not an easy task and it requires dedicated resources of manpower, system and budget. Any lapse from company would result in decrease of market share and profit.

Positioning and Differentiating the Market Offering Through Product Life Cycle

Today's markets represent the surplus market, with a wide range of product available for sell. Consumer has huge product offering to choose from, for soap, there are more than dozen brands and each brand has at least 4 or 5 varieties. Companies have to work on strategies, which would differentiate their products from competitors. This differentiation strategy also cannot last for long as competition is likely to catch very soon. Companies are aware of the product life cycle; challenge is to work up strategies for positioning and differentiating as to extend product life and making it profitable.

A market place has many segments out of which companies have to make a choice in which to operate. And within the market segment companies need to decide its offering and image. This process of identifying and build the brand image within a segment as to occupy presence in consumer mind is called positioning. Positioning is all about consumers rather than the product, the challenge is to develop a positive perception in consumer mind. Positioning is done based on an idea the product promotes, too many ideas will confuse the customer. Companies need to decide which idea to promote to be ahead of competition. Positioning should offer clarity to customer about what product is all about. For example, a competitor has similar positioning ideas, than the company is better positioning product where it enjoys a competitive advantage. Now, it is up to the marketing plan to create programs which highlight this positioning idea.

Positioning related marketing programs are responsible to pass unique selling proposition on to the customer. However, this can be taken forward with differentiation. Differentiation is process of adding more meaning to the product by highlighting attributes beyond the central theme. Task of differentiation is to highlight the relevant benefits in a distinctive manner which cannot be easily followed by competitors and provide profitable benefits to the company.

There are many differentiation tools available to the company to extract maximum benefits. The main variables which offer differentiation are product, service, personnel, channel and image. Product related attributes serve a good base of the differentiation. However, product differentiation varies depending on the nature of industry. For example, commodity products are difficult to differentiate on appearance where as automobiles present an opportunity with plenty of differentiations.

Service plays important differentiation tool where differentiation is difficult based on physical attributes of product. Differentiation in service can be achieved based on ordering ease, customer service during the sell, after sell customer service and consulting. One step forward in service is differentiation by personnel. By exhibiting a professional, reliable, quick and courteous response to customer can differentiate companies from competitors.

The distribution channel plays its part as differentiation tool and can prove to be competitive advantage. For example Dell computer through direct selling approach delivers computer system right at door step of home owners and offices.

Another important differentiation tool is image. There are various ways to achieve image differentiation depending on industry and market segment. Sponsoring of event and causes is one way building up image among consumers.

As pointed out earlier, company's strategy has to change according to the stage in the product life cycle. The product life has introduction stage, growth stage, maturity stage and saturation stage. In introduction stage focus is on establishing a foothold in the market space and consumer mind, through promotion, product trial and establishing distribution channel. In growth stage, sales are increasing and company is striving for the number one space. Strategies here consist of acquiring new customer, expansion brand line and fighting of competition. In maturation stage, growth is not explosive as before, there are no further distributors to add and sales start a decline. Here companies attempt to streamline product category, enter new markets and modify product feature as well as attributes. In saturation stage, it is time for companies to review sustainability of product by conducting the cost benefit analysis and remove products, which are dragging on company's profitability.

Markets in which companies are operating too have similar phases as products. Companies have to analyze positioning and differentiating strategies at various stages of the product and market life cycle.

Dear Readers,
I, Thank You, for supporting and reading my book.
Hope your wishes will inspire me to write more such
books in future.
Regards,

Sourav Das